MINDST
Level 1

CHERRY LAKE PUBLISHING • ANN ARBOR, MICHIGAN   by Rena Hixon

CHERRY
LAKE
Publishing

A Note to Adults: Please review the instructions for the activities in this book before allowing children to do them. Be sure to help them with any activities you do not think they can safely complete on their own.

A Note to Kids: Be sure to ask an adult for help with these activities when you need it. Always put your safety first!

Published in the United States of America by Cherry Lake Publishing
Ann Arbor, Michigan
www.cherrylakepublishing.com

Reading Adviser: Marla Conn, Read With Me Now
Photo Credits: Cover and pages 1, 4, 5, and 16, ©AP Images; page 8, ©Ekaterina_Minaeva/Shutterstock.com; page 9, Eirik Refsdal/tinyurl.com/o4fu8h7/CC BY 2.0; pages 10, 11, 12, 13, 17, 20, 21, 23, and 26, Rena Hixon; page 15, Iwan Gabovitch/tinyurl.com/nnv5wz5/CC BY 2.0; page 24, ©Lisa Werner/Alamy

Library of Congress Cataloging-in-Publication Data
Hixon, Rena, author.
  Mindstorms. Level 1 / by Rena Hixon.
    pages cm. — (21st century skills innovation library. Unofficial guides)
  Audience: Grades 4 to 6.
  Includes bibliographical references and index.
  ISBN 978-1-63470-524-0 (lib. bdg.) — ISBN 978-1-63470-644-5 (pbk.) — ISBN 978-1-63470-584-4 (pdf) — ISBN 978-1-63470-704-6 (ebook)
1. LEGO Mindstorms toys—Juvenile literature. 2. Robotics—Juvenile literature. 3. Computer programming—Juvenile literature. I. Title.
  TJ211.2.H484 2016
  629.8'92—dc23   2015028525

Cherry Lake Publishing would like to acknowledge the work of The Partnership for 21st Century Skills. Please visit www.p21.org for more information.

Printed in the United States of America
Corporate Graphics
January 2016

Contents

Chapter 1

What Is Lego Mindstorms?

Have you ever wanted to bring your Lego creations to life? Or to build a robot that can walk? Wouldn't it be incredible for that Lego truck you built to drive around on its own? With the help of Lego Mindstorms, you can make these ideas and many others a reality.

You can build amazing things using Mindstorms.

An expert builder shows off some of the many robots that can be created using a Mindstorms EV3 kit.

A Mindstorms kit comes with motors, **sensors**, and a programmable computer. These can be combined with standard Lego pieces to build robots that sense their environment and react to it. This means Mindstorms robots can follow set paths or even travel on their own while avoiding objects. The best part of these projects is that they are easily accomplished once you learn how to work with the Mindstorms system.

There have been three versions of Lego Mindstorms released so far. With each one, creators have made changes and improvements to the earlier versions. The biggest difference between the

A Fun Way to Learn

One of the purposes of Lego Mindstorms is to help kids learn the basics of **engineering** and science. Engineers are people who design everything from computers and cell phones to vehicles and bridges. Working with Mindstorms robots is a great first step toward learning how to be an engineer. For example, building a Mindstorms car will teach you a lot about how real cars work.

kits is the programmable computer brick. The first kit released contained a brick called the RCX (Remote Command Execution). The building system was more like the standard bricks that Lego originally sold. The next brick was the NXT (Next Generation). The most recent brick is the EV3 (Evolution 3). Both the NXT and EV3 bricks are used with Lego Technic building pieces rather than the standard brick construction. This change was made to improve the sturdiness of the designs.

There are two types of kits to choose from for each version of Mindstorms. One is the retail kit, and the other is the education kit. The education kits are designed mainly for use in schools. They include more parts than retail kits. For example, the retail EV3 kit comes with three sensors, while the education kit comes with five sensors.

Different **software** has been released for each version of Lego Mindstorms. For the RCX, there are two main software packages: Robolab and RIS. The NXT software is called NXTg. The software for the EV3 is simply called EV3 software. The software is used to program your robots. It uses a graphical **interface** where you drag and drop **icons** to form your program.

There will be many references to "the kit" throughout this book. This will always mean the EV3 Mindstorms kit, which is the most recent version of Mindstorms.

The Lego Company believes that kids should learn using hands-on methods. This means discovering new things on your own as you work on Mindstorms projects. As you go through the rest of this book, there will be activities for you to try. Before you read the solutions, try finding the answers to the questions!

Chapter 2

Learning the Parts

L earning the names of the Mindstorms parts will help you understand how each one is used. They can be divided into five main categories: bricks, plates, Technic pieces, electric pieces, and other pieces.

Any standard Lego pieces can be used along with the Mindstorms kit.

Bricks are the traditional Lego pieces with studs that snap together. The studs are the bumps on top of the pieces.

Plates have the same studs as bricks. However, they are only one-third as thick as a standard brick.

Technic pieces are special Lego parts that are used for building technical creations such as Mars rovers and robots. Some Technic pieces are shaped like pins and **axles**. Others look like standard plates and bricks with holes in them.

The various wires, motors, and sensors in a Mindstorms kit belong to the electric pieces category. They are the parts that will bring your creations to life.

Sensors allow your Mindstorms creations to see and hear what is going on around them.

The rest of the pieces don't fit neatly into the other four categories. However, they still play a very important role in the building process.

Bricks and plates are named based on how many studs they have. Each is described using two numbers. For example, a 2 x 3 brick is two studs wide and three studs long. Below you see examples of different sizes of standard Lego bricks. Some of the bricks have round edges, some have sloped edges, and some have sharp corners. The EV3 kit does not come with any standard bricks. However, any Lego pieces available can be used with it.

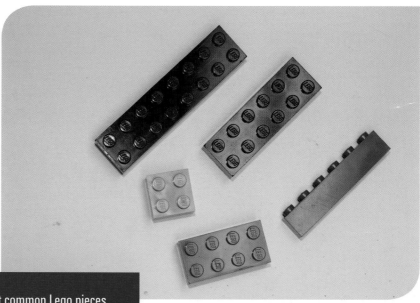

Bricks are some of the most common Lego pieces.

The main colors in Mindstorms kits are black and gray. There are also a few blue, yellow, and green pieces. You can add different colors by combining other Lego sets with your Mindstorms creations.

Plates are sized the same way as bricks. When needed, they can be stacked together to form the same height as a brick. Three plates stacked on top of each other make the height of a regular brick. Below are some examples of standard plates.

Special plates, such as plate corners, flat plates, and plates with holes, are shown on page 12.

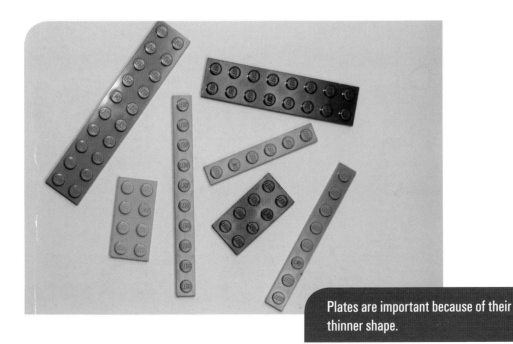

Plates are important because of their thinner shape.

Gearing Up

Technic pieces include a variety of gears. These round pieces have ridges called teeth around their edges. They can lock together in complex arrangements and make each other spin in different directions. This allows you to create many types of machines.

Gears are more than just Mindstorms pieces. You can find them inside everything from watches to cars. Learning how they work in Mindstorms projects could help you understand how to work on more complicated objects one day.

Technic pieces make up the majority of a Mindstorms kit. They can be divided into different categories of their own. Technic pieces include axles, gears, pins, connectors, and plates and bricks

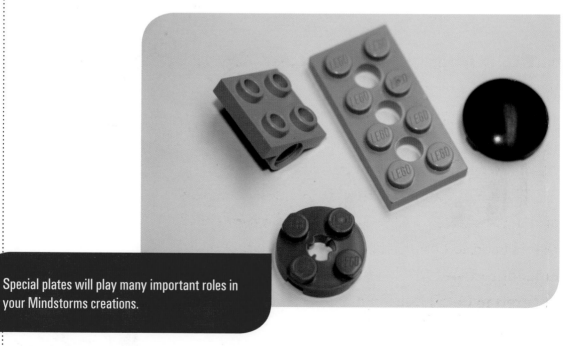

Special plates will play many important roles in your Mindstorms creations.

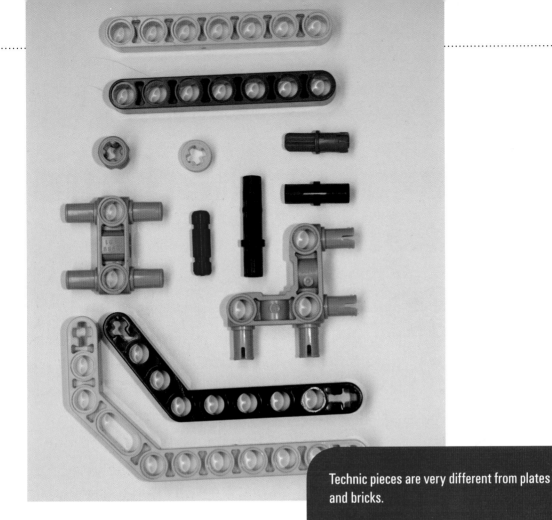

Technic pieces are very different from plates and bricks.

with holes for use with axles and pins. Wheels and tires are also included in this category. As with standard pieces, the size of the plates and bricks are measured by studs. Above and on page 12 are some common Technic pieces.

The electric pieces are the EV3 brick, motors, and sensors. The EV3 contains a **microprocessor** that is used to control the other electric pieces. It is considered the "brain" of the kit. These pieces will be covered in detail later in this book.

Chapter 3

Understanding the EV3 Brick

To get started with your own Mindstorms projects, you will need to learn how to use the programmable EV3 brick.

There are eight main **ports** on the EV3. Four of them are **output** ports. These are where you will connect motors to the EV3. The output ports are located on the end of the brick above the display screen. They are labeled A, B, C, and D. You will use these labels when programming the EV3.

The EV3 also has four **input** ports. These are located on the end of the EV3 below the display screen. They are labeled 1, 2, 3, and 4. Like the output ports, they play an important role in programming the EV3. The input ports take readings from various types of sensors. Different Mindstorms kits come with different sensors. Additional sensors can be purchased or built to work with the EV3. There is also a built-in rotation sensor inside each motor.

The programmable EV3 brick will be the core of all your Mindstorms creations.

The EV3 has an LCD screen that is used to display information. It has six buttons. The dark gray button in the middle turns on the EV3. The four arrow buttons around the middle button are used to scroll between options on the display. The gray button to the left underneath the display is used to back out of menu screens and to turn off the EV3.

Turn on the EV3 and observe the display. While the EV3 is powering on, the screen will read "Mindstorms starting." The lights on the brick will turn green when the EV3 is ready to use.

Press the center button to turn on the EV3.

One of the things you should observe on the screen is an icon at the very top that shows the battery status. To the left of the battery icon is the EV3's name. The **default** is "EV3," so that's what you should see if nobody has changed it.

There are four main icons on the EV3 screen. You can choose between them using the buttons on the brick. The first one is an arrow in a circle. When this icon is selected, it shows the most recently used programs. This will let you quickly load programs that you have used in the past.

The second icon looks like a piece of paper. This is the program symbol. Selecting it will show all the projects that have been loaded on the EV3. If you select a project, you will see all the programs associated with that project. You will find out more about projects and programs later in this book.

The next icon has six small circles at the top. If you select it, you can do some basic programming on the brick itself without going back to your computer. Once you start to learn the Mindstorms programming language, you will see how useful this feature can be.

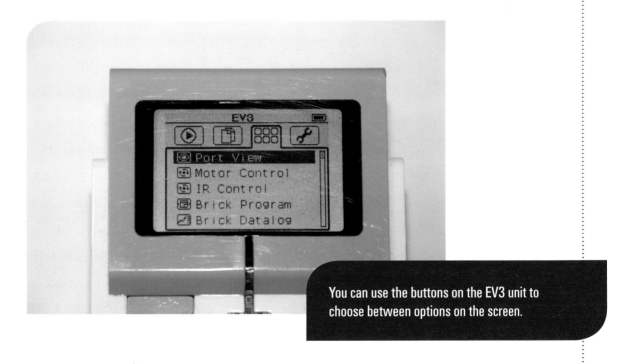

You can use the buttons on the EV3 unit to choose between options on the screen.

Processors Everywhere

One of the most important parts of the EV3 brick is its microprocessor. This small computer can be programmed to do many different things. Despite their small size, microprocessors can be used to control even the most complex devices. Everything from a calculator and printer to a laptop computer and cell phone contains its own microprocessor.

One thing you are going to want to use a lot in this section is the Port View. If you select Port View, you can view the status of all the ports that have motors or sensors attached.

The last icon is a tool symbol. By selecting it, you can change the volume of the brick's speaker and the amount of time before the brick will go to sleep. You can also turn Bluetooth and Wi-Fi on or off and find out more information about your EV3 unit.

The most common way to program the EV3 is to plug it into a computer. There is a small port labeled "PC" on the EV3 unit. It is located on the same side as the output ports. You can plug one end of a USB cable into this port and the other end into your computer. This will allow the computer to exchange information with the EV3.

Chapter 4

An Introduction to Programming

To effectively use your EV3, you need to know how to program it. You will do this using the EV3 software. There are two versions of the software. One is a free version that can be downloaded from the Mindstorms Web site. The other is an education version, which you must buy. The education version comes with some advanced features. However, the free version gives you everything you need to get started.

Download the free version of the software from *www.lego.com/en-us/mindstorms/downloads/download-software*. Choose the right version for the type of computer you have. After you have downloaded and installed the software, you will see an icon on your computer labeled "Lego Mindstorms EV3 software." Double-click it to open the program.

Once you have opened the EV3 software, you should see a + sign. Click on it to start a new project. A project is a collection of programs. You can name the project, and you can name the programs in the project. This allows you to have related programs in a project. When you add a new project, the software automatically opens a new program for you.

Once you have opened a program, you should see six different colors at the bottom of the screen. For basic programs, you will use the first two colors: green and orange. If you move your mouse over the icons under the green tab, you should see "Medium Motor", "Large Motor", "Move Steering", "Move Tank", "Display", "Sound", and "Brick Status Light". You will use these to control the motors, display, sound, and lights on the brick.

To test the inputs, you are going to use the icons under the orange tab. If you mouse over those icons, you should see "Wait", "Loop", "Switch", and "Loop Interrupt".

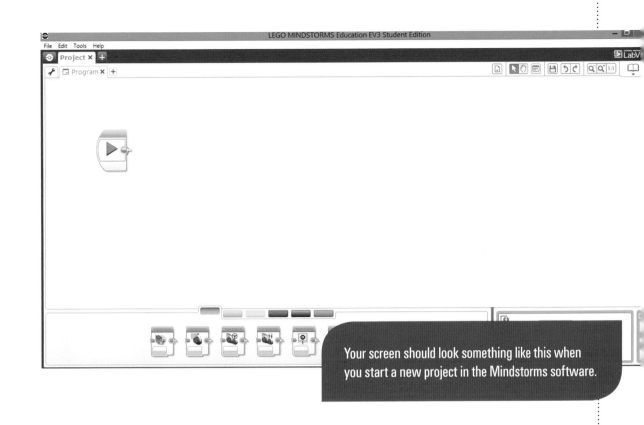

Your screen should look something like this when you start a new project in the Mindstorms software.

To get familiar with programming, start by using the "Sound" icon under the green tab. Put your mouse over this icon, then click and drag it into the programming space. You will need to attach it to the green "Start" icon that is already there.

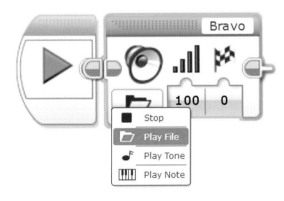

Programming Like a Pro

Using the EV3 software will help you learn the basics of computer programming. Programming is the process of creating instructions for a computer to do different things. This involves using special languages that computers can understand.

The main difference between programming an EV3 and programming a regular computer is that the EV3 uses a programming language based on icons. This makes it easier to learn than traditional programming languages, which are text based.

There are three tabs you can click on the "Sound" icon. The first one on the left gives the options to "Stop", "Play File", "Play Tone", and "Play Note". The easiest to use first is "Play File". Once you make that selection, you need to position your cursor over the white box at the top right corner of the screen. Choose any of the Lego sound files to listen to the different sounds the EV3 can make using this icon. Congratulations—you've created a simple program!

To load the program onto the EV3 brick, be sure the EV3 is connected to the computer. At the bottom right corner of the computer screen, you should see a downward arrow with dashes. Click on it to send your program to the EV3. If you select the sideways arrow underneath the downward one, it will load your program and immediately run it. Be careful not to use this button if you turn the motors on in your program. You might cause your EV3 to fall off a table!

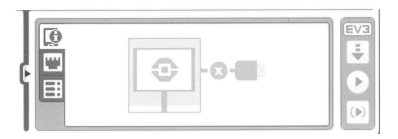

Another fun way to use the software is to view images on the EV3 display. Under the green software tab, choose a "Display" icon and attach it to the "Start" icon in your program. On the icon is a picture of the EV3 buttons. Under that icon, there are four selections. Select "Image". You will use the top right corner white space again to select your image. Under "Lego image files," you will find many images that can be displayed on your EV3 brick. Choose one, then load the new program onto your EV3.

Chapter 5

Locomotion

N ow that you understand the basic idea behind creating programs, it is time to learn about locomotion. Locomotion is the way something moves from place to place. There are many different kinds of locomotion, from walking or running to rolling on wheels. Mindstorms creations can use several different kinds of locomotion. In this chapter, you will learn how to use the kit's motors to make a robot car move forward and backward and make turns.

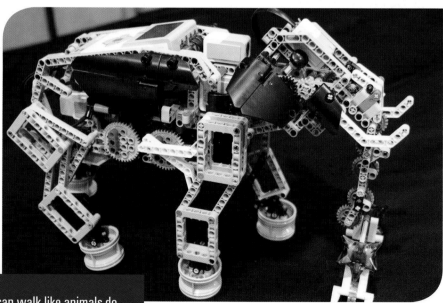

Some Mindstorms robots can walk like animals do.

Visit *www.damienkee.com/home/2013/8/2/ rileyrover-ev3-classroom-robot-design.html* to get directions for building a simple Mindstorms car. In this particular design, the wires for the motors are crossed. For this activity, do not cross the wires. Each motor should be connected to the port closest to it.

There are different ways to program your car to turn. Turns can be made with one motor going forward and one motor reversed, or with one motor going forward and the other motor stopped. Turns can also be made by slowing down one motor. The object of this activity is for you to understand how to make a robot turn in the correct direction and the differences between types of turns.

The floor surface you use can make a big difference when doing this experiment. A non-carpeted floor will allow the robot to turn better and is recommended for this experiment. Carpet provides more resistance. This makes it more difficult for the car to turn.

The EV3 supplies the power to turn the motors through the output ports (B and C in this case). When programming the motors, a negative number creates backward movement and a positive number creates forward movement.

First, write a program that will make the car move forward. Start by putting a "Move Tank" icon in your program. When you bring in the icon, the default under the motors will be 50. Leave that as it is. Under the # symbol, which stands for rotations, change the 1 to a 5. See the program below.

Download the program to your EV3. Place the car on the floor and run the program. Have someone ready to catch the runaway car. What happens? What is causing the robot to go in the direction it is going? It is going forward because you told the motors to move in the forward direction with your program.

Your final program should look something like this.

Back in your program, change the numbers underneath each motor from 50 to –50. How will this affect your car's movement? Download the program and run it. The car should have gone backward.

Now you can program your car to turn. In your program, change motor B to 0 and motor C to 50. Download and run the program. The robot should turn right and move round and round in a circle.

Change your program to set motor B to 50 and motor C to 0. The robot should now turn in a circle to the left.

Now put motor B in reverse and motor C in the forward direction by using –50 for B and 50 for C. (Remember negative numbers mean backward.) What does your robot do now? How is it different than when you had one motor on and one off? It should still turn left, but it should move much faster.

In the program, put motor C in reverse and motor B in forward. You should be able to predict this one. It should turn right at the same speed the previous program turned left.

You should notice by now that your car will turn any time there is a difference in speed between the two motors. The closer the values of the motors, the slower the car will turn. By making one motor 40 and one 50, you will see the robot veer off in the direction of the slower motor without turning sharply. If you make one motor 50 and one −10, the car will turn even quicker than it does with one motor turned off.

For the last part of this activity, you need to mark a course on the floor using masking tape or electrical tape. It should be 10 feet (3 meters) long. Put a piece of tape 2 to 3 feet (61 to 91 centimeters) long on the floor. Measure 10 feet (3 m) and place another piece of tape the same length **parallel** to the first one.

You are going to time your robot. Set up the car a little behind the first line of tape. Start a stopwatch when the car's front wheels cross the first line. Stop timing when the car's front wheels touch the second line. Write down the time in a notebook. Readings should be in seconds and hundredths of seconds. Time the car at least three times to make sure your measurements are about the same each time. If there are big differences between the measurements, you should repeat the process. It is most likely that you made a mistake with the stopwatch.

Now you will get an idea of how power levels affect a robot's movement. The default power level

Get Creative!

Now that you have a grasp of the basics of Mindstorms, try creating some of your own inventions. Experiment with motors and programs. See what happens when you try different things. Even if a project doesn't turn out the way you plan, you will probably learn something new. As you try different things, you will become a Mindstorms expert little by little. What will you build next?

is 50 for each motor. Put the "Move Tank" icon in a program. Change the number of rotations to 100 and the power level to 100.

As already described, run your robot and observe how long it takes to go 10 feet (3 m). Change your power level to 50 and try it. Now try power level 30. You should notice a big difference in the times.

In this book, you have learned some basics about the EV3, some basic programming, and how to make the robot move and turn. This is an important first step on the road to becoming a Mindstorms master. Are you ready to move forward and start working with sensors? Try the next book in this series!

Glossary

axles (AK-sulz) rods in the center of wheels, around which the wheels turn

default (di-FAWLT) a setting or option that will be effective if you don't specifically choose one in a computer program

engineering (en-juh-NEER-ing) the process of designing and building machines or large structures

icons (EYE-kahnz) graphic symbols on a computer screen that represent programs, functions, or files

input (IN-put) information fed into a computer

interface (IN-tur-fase) the system used to interact with a computer or other device

microprocessor (mye-kroh-PRAH-ses-ur) a computer chip that controls the functions of an electronic device

output (OUT-put) information produced by a computer

parallel (PAR-uh-lel) staying the same distance from each other and never crossing or meeting

ports (PORTS) places on a computer that are designed for a particular kind of plug

sensors (SEN-surz) devices that measure light, sound, movement, and touch

software (SAWFT-wair) computer programs that control the workings of the equipment, or hardware, and direct it to do specific tasks

Find Out More

BOOKS

Karch, Marziah. *Build and Program Your Own Lego Mindstorms EV3 Robots*. Indianapolis: Que Publishing, 2014.

Rollins, Mark. *Beginning Lego Mindstorms EV3*. New York: Apress, 2014.

Valk, Laurens. *The LEGO MINDSTORMS EV3 Discovery Book: A Beginner's Guide to Building and Programming Robots*. San Francisco: No Starch Press, 2014.

WEB SITE

Lego Mindstorms: Build a Robot

www.lego.com/en-us/mindstorms/build-a-robot
Check out instructions for building other Mindstorms robots.

Index

About the Author

Rena Hixon received a bachelor's degree in computer science from the University of Missouri–Rolla (now Missouri University of Science and Technology). She also earned a doctorate in electrical engineering from Wichita State University. She worked as a software design engineer for 11 years and has taught computer science classes at Wichita State for more than 13 years. In 2004, Rena and her husband started a Lego robotics club for homeschooled students. Its aim is to teach engineering principles, emphasizing math and science, to children. Rena has also taught her own Lego robotics camps for 12 years as well as camps at Missouri S&T for several years.